BIGGEST VS. SMALLEST
THINGS WITH WINGS

Susan K. Mitchell

CONTENTS

Big vs. Small

There are many types of animals with wings. Some are huge birds. Others are tiny insects so small they can barely be seen. There is even a mammal in the mix! No matter their size, they are all amazing opposites.

WORDS TO KNOW

gizzard—A muscular stomach pouch that helps birds grind up food.

incubate—To keep eggs warm so they can hatch.

mammals—Warm-blooded animals with hair or fur.

rain forest—A forest area that gets a huge amount of rainfall each year.

GOING BATTY

Flying foxes are not foxes at all. They are bats. In fact, they are the biggest bats in the world! One of the largest is the giant golden-crowned flying fox.

The flying fox is BIG!

The bumblebee bat is SMALL!

The smallest bat in the world is the bumblebee bat. It is tiny enough to fit on a human thumb. This bat is also one of the tiniest of all **mammals.**

The giant golden-crowned flying fox lives in the Philippines. From wing tip to wing tip can be five feet across. Its body can be twelve inches long. It can weigh about three pounds. These huge bats live in caves. They also live in the **rain forest**.

Fast Fact

There are very few bumblebee bats.

Thailand is the only place the bumblebee bat lives. It is only a little over one inch long. It weighs about as much as a dime. The bats live in limestone caves.

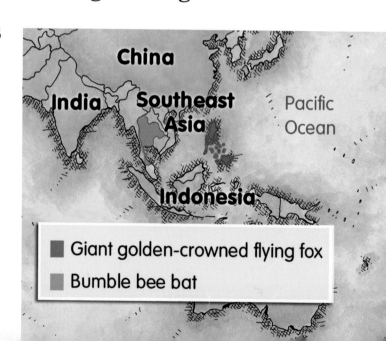

China

India   Southeast   Pacific
        Asia   Ocean

Indonesia

■ Giant golden-crowned flying fox
■ Bumble bee bat

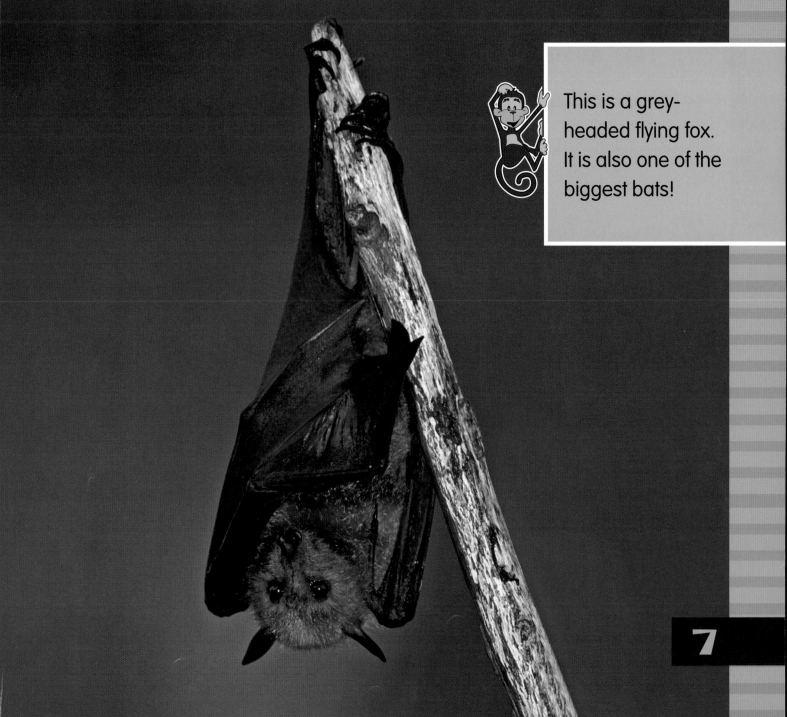

This is a grey-headed flying fox. It is also one of the biggest bats!

Like all bats, the giant golden-crowned flying fox is a mammal. They have furry bodies. These huge bats are fruit eaters. Their favorite fruits are figs. At night, they may fly up to thirty miles to search for fruit to eat.

The bumblebee bat is an insect eater. Its favorite food is small flies. These tiny bats only leave their caves for about an hour each day. The bumblebee bat can hover in one place as it flies.

Fast Fact

A flying fox has a pointed snout and large eyes. This makes it look like a fox.

These bumblebee bats hang upside down in a cave.

AMAZING MOTHS

2

It is a bird! It is a bat! No, it is the atlas moth. This huge moth is often mistaken for a small bat or bird when it flies. It is the largest moth in the world.

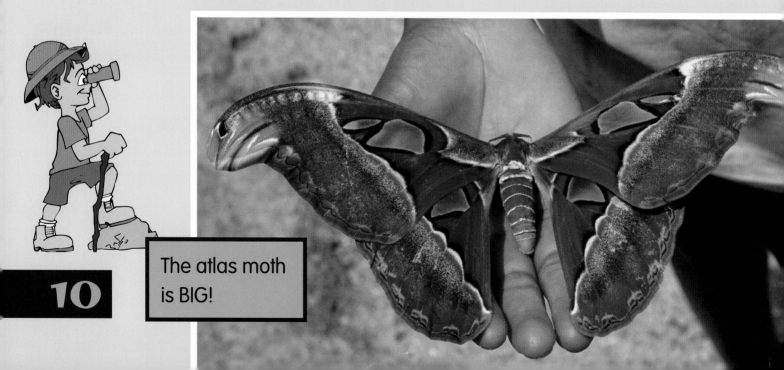

The atlas moth is BIG!

The smallest moths in the world belong to the pygmy moth family. The word *pygmy* means small. The name for this group of moths is *Nepticulid* (nep-TIC-cue-lid). There are many types of pygmy moths.

The pygmy moth is SMALL!

11

The atlas moth has a wingspan of up to twelve inches. The females are larger than the males. They live all over Southeast Asia.

The tiny pygmy moths can be found all over the world. The only place they do not live is Antarctica.

The atlas moth has a wingspan of up to twelve inches. That is as big as a dinner plate!

Fast Fact

In Taiwan, people sometimes use atlas moth cocoons as purses. In India, people make a special silk from the cocoons.

Atlas moth caterpillars grow quickly. They may reach more than four inches long. They eat citrus and evergreen leaves. Adult atlas moths do not eat at all. They do not even have mouths! They only live two weeks.

Pygmy moths are leaf miners. This means the caterpillars live inside leaves. They only eat the inner layers of the leaf. This can cause much damage to a plant.

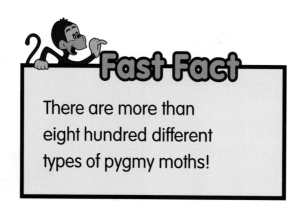

Fast Fact

There are more than eight hundred different types of pygmy moths!

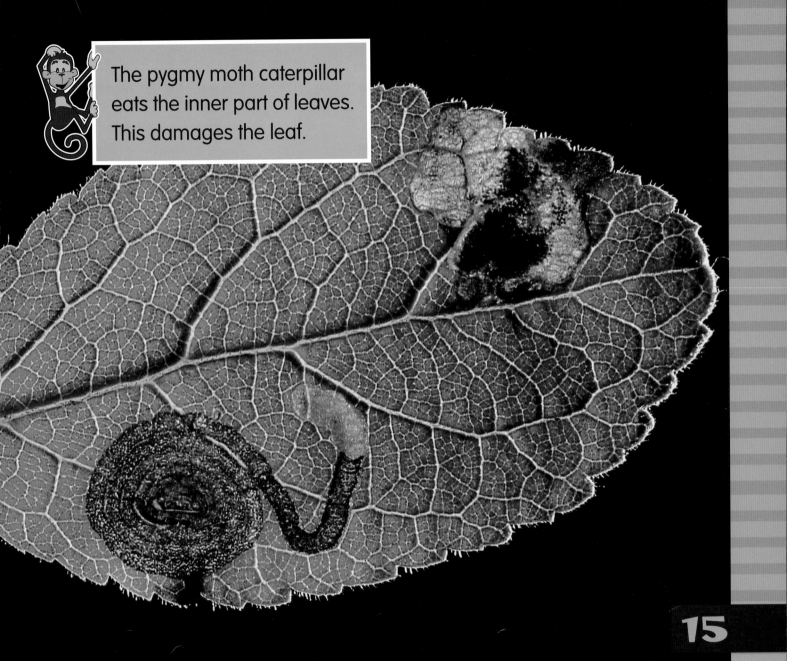

The pygmy moth caterpillar eats the inner part of leaves. This damages the leaf.

BIRDS OF A FEATHER

The biggest thing with wings cannot fly. It is the ostrich. But this huge bird can run very fast. It can reach speeds of forty-three miles per hour!

The ostrich is BIG!

The tiny bee hummingbird is the smallest bird in the world. It has wings that move very fast. They beat eighty times each second. The wings move so fast the bee hummingbird can hover in one place.

The bee hummingbird is SMALL!

17

Africa is home to the ostrich. The male ostrich grows to be between seven and nine feet tall. Ostriches' legs are very powerful. They have a four-inch claw on each foot. Their kick is powerful enough to kill a lion.

Bee hummingbirds live in Cuba. They only grow to be about two inches long. They weigh less than a penny. The males are smaller than the females. Their hearts beat very fast. But they cannot fly long distances.

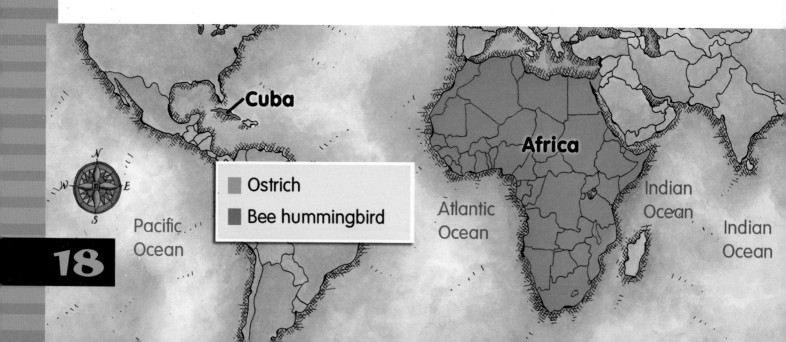

Cuba

Africa

Indian Ocean

Atlantic Ocean

Pacific Ocean

Indian Ocean

N
W — E
S

■	Ostrich
■	Bee hummingbird

Fast Fact

An ostrich sometimes eats weird things. It may eat sand or rocks. These help grind up food in its **gizzard**.

The nest of the bee hummingbird is about the size of the coin next to it. The Cuban coin is about the size of a U.S. quarter.

An ostrich egg is the biggest egg in the world. It weighs about three pounds. Male ostriches often help females hatch their eggs. They take turns lying on the eggs to **incubate** them.

The bee hummingbird has one of the smallest nests in the world. It is less than an inch across. They also lay the smallest eggs. Each egg is only half an inch long.

Fast Fact

Bee hummingbirds drink plant nectar. They also eat small insects. These tiny birds have to drink eight times their body mass each day. They also eat half their weight each day.

An ostrich egg (right) is BIG! A chicken egg is on the left.

MANY YEARS AGO...

The largest bird that ever lived is the **extinct** giant moa. It lived in New Zealand. The giant moa stood more than eleven feet tall. Like the ostrich, it could not fly.

The heaviest bird in the world is the extinct elephant bird. It lived in Madagascar, an island off the coast of Africa. This bird was shorter than the giant moa. But it was much heavier. It weighed more than one thousand pounds!

The giant moa lived many, many years ago on New Zealand.

LEARN MORE

Books

Jango-Cohen, Judith. *Hovering Hummingbirds.* Minneapolis, Minn.: Lerner Publishing Group, 2002.

Jenkins, Steve. *Actual Size.* Boston: Houghton-Mifflin, 2004.

Wheeler, Jill C. *Bumblebee Bats.* Edina, Minn.: Checkerboard Books, 2005.

Internet Addresses

On the Move: Fantastic Fliers
<http://magma.nationalgeographic.com/ngexplorer/0703/articles/mainarticle.html>

Organization for Bat Conservation
<http://www.batconservation.org/content/Kidsandbats.html>

iNDEX

Bailey Books

an imprint of

Enslow Publishers, Inc.

40 Industrial Road
Box 398
Berkeley Heights, NJ 07922
USA

http://www.enslow.com

These books are dedicated to the students of Greentree.

Bailey Books, an imprint of Enslow Publishers, Inc.

Copyright © 2011 by Enslow Publishers, Inc.

Library of Congress Cataloging-in-Publication Data

Mitchell, Susan K.

  Biggest vs. smallest things with wings / Susan K. Mitchell.

    p. cm. — (Biggest vs. smallest animals)

  Includes bibliographical references and index.

  Summary: "Provides information on the biggest and smallest bats, moths, and birds"—Provided by publisher.

  ISBN 978-0-7660-3578-2

  1. Bats—Juvenile literature. 2. Moths—Juvenile literature. 3. Birds—Juvenile literature. 4. Animal flight—Juvenile literature. 5. Body size—Juvenile literature. I. Title. II. Title: Biggest versus smallest things with wings.

  QL737.C5M68 2010

  590—dc22

2009001679

Printed in the United States of America

062010 Lake Book Manufacturing, Inc., Melrose Park, IL

10 9 8 7 6 5 4 3 2 1

Illustration Credits: Ingo Arndt/Minden Pictures, pp. 1 (small), 11; © 1999 Artville, LLC, pp. 12, 18; Bernard Castelein/naturepl.com, p. 4; Gyorgy Csoka, Hungary Forest Research Institute, Bugwood.org, p. 15; Steve Downer/ardea.com, p. 9; Enslow Publishers, Inc., illustrations of monk and children throughout the book; Museum of New Zealand Te Papa Tongarewa/The Bridgeman Art Library International, p. 22; NHPA/Lee Dalton, pp. 17, 19; NHPA/Martin Harvey, p. 13; NHP Daniel Heuclin, pp. 1 (big), 10; Richard T. Nowitz/Photo Researchers, Inc., p. 21; Dr. Merlin D. Tuttle/Photo Researchers, Inc., p. 5; Visuals Unlimited, Inc., pp. 7, 16, back cover.

Cover Illustration: NHPA/Daniel Heuclin (giant atlas moth) and Ingo Arndt/Minden Pictures (pygmy moth).